BESPOKE MOMENTS

OF A SERENE HEART

SWETA SRIVASTAVA

Bespoke Moments
By: Sweta Srivastava

Published by Paper2publish (Manan Verma)
Jwalapur, Uttarakhand, 249407
www.paper2publish.com
www.mananverma.com

ISBN: 978-93-94450-29-5

Help and Supported by Paper2Publish
www.paper2publish.com

TABLE OF CONTENTS

TRIBUTE

My book "Bespoke moments- of a serene heart" is a tribute to my parents, My father Lt. Col N .M Saksena , whose courage, wisdom and dedication has inspired me always and my mother Mrs. Vinita Saksena , for all that my life has turned out to be.

My parents are no longer with me as I take on to writing my very first composition, but they are the ones who carefully and meticulously enabled me to put my thoughts into words ,empowered me with an education, which strings my beliefs and perceptions into poems and it is their blessings which have allowed me to have the moments about which I have written in my book. I wish I could have shared this joy with you!

PROLOGUE

"Fill your paper with the breathings of your heart."

-William Wordsworth

In the journey of life, we all scribble through our thoughts, some have a gift to put their emotions to ink ,and for me, I distinctly remember when I started writing, it was through the images I captured to mark as a memento ,of a place I travelled to ,or simply as a remembrance of a feeling that made me long for more.And so, my breathings started ,mostly in form of small videos that I would capture,learning nuances of editing and completing with captions.

Little did I realise then that the process was as if I was thinking through my fingers,yet speaking from my heart.With each small project I completed typing, I wanted to go back to my gallery and see it once more. In my own personal space,I received that prizing which motivated me to believe that I must try to write.

Like most maiden authors would feel, words to me comes naturally,but my family and my friends,the small group with whom I shared my poetry have become that reason that I have made this attempt to print my gamut of emotions, mostly as free verses ,that is almost a resounding catharsis.

BESPOKE MOMENTS

Dear readers,

Have you ever believed, that whatever comes across your way has a reason ? Life is not only about waking up each morning to see yourself engrossed in the everyday designs. Each day is there also to celebrate what it brings to you. As the sun rises it brings light, when it is atop the horizon it brings warmth ,when it has done the day, it adds more colours to the sky and when it sets,have you ever seen if there was no light?

So in the darkness you see the most precious emotions, because when the moon rises, it's a bit shy, as it takes its waxing gibbous form,when the night presses, its silver brightens like shimmers in the twilight,when its time again for a new day to begin, its crescent forms like a shadow below a cloud.Cherish the dark because ,if it was never a night ,could we ever see that the moon too has scars?

And the clouds now cover the azure , hiding behind the sun and the moon! Drifting afar with the western winds,at first they are a fluff of mist ,but when they become dense,the clouds are the heralds of joy.The clouds have rained now ,and a days cycle may

begin soon,but dear friends,have you ever wondered if there wasn't this overshadow,would we have ever seen the rainbow?
A spectrum forms in the myraid hues of this rainbow. The prism etches a curve along the skyline,from one corner as you start to see you find puddles of water ,since it rained last night,look a little further and you can find the aureole forcing you to close your eyes,and looking up again when you turn to see its far end,the variegation plunges into a mystery ,but if there was no rainbow ,do you think we could ever marvel this life ?

All of this in my everyday life has been my Bespoke Moments ,which I celebrate through my poetry,each poem reflecting a part of my fondness to ink what paths I tread,which sights I see and how it strengthens my conviction ,that yes! everything happens for a reason.

-SWETA

A SERENE HEART

Early in my years I realized that I was living a rebellious childhood. No, my life wasn't going through pains and anxieties or it wasn't where I was living a suppressed life. Perhaps it was an innate thing, which always made me think different, than how it was supposed to be thought of, I accepted what I wished to and i did all that made me happy. In the` same years I realized that the world isn't always very accepting of unconventional thoughts, the sagacity led to compunction and I watched myself change into a serene heart….

I learnt through the changes I had made ,my life was tranquil like the waters in a lake, it was calm as a breeze and soft as feather , but my heart had an omniscient vehemence as a whole .I spent my years fascinated by the splendor of the world, adoring the facades of enticing deeds of what people did, or how they spoke, it all began to set into my hearts contentment and my once fragile heart is now enveloped in a tranquility .Even I find it more amicable and faithful to be calm in life.

As in now, this softness has been a bliss, just like when you breathe deeply and slowly, your heart beat starts to synchronize with the rhythm of your breathing, the same way every feeling I have pondered on has been a chain-link to how I anticipate this sphere to be. It feels but wonderful to be at ease with oneself and to be in competition with just no one. That is what I am made up of, candid but composed.

A heart that appears to be quiet is not often the most silent one, when it comes to discerning what surrounds it. In fact, it is indelicate for the reason that it apprehends what is said but doesn't disguise how it manifests. If one is quiet and free from disturbances, I can say definitely that the person is on the qui vive towards a passionate road. I have come to the conclusion that being silent does not mean that you haven't felt defiant ever, but it's just that you become the depth of the lake, persistence of the breeze and the far reaching strength of the feathers in the wings, I spoke about earlier. It's not just an aura or a mirage in the desert, and so I accept to be called a Serene Heart.

- **SWETA**

FOREWORD

By

Ex Principal, Army Public School, Akhnoor
Director Academic IDPS Akhnoor J&K

I am overwhelmed to extend my feelings through message to extend my gratitude to Mrs Sweta Srivastava ,an excellent teacher, balanced personality, wonderful writer, poet of nature and very caring and child friendly educationist .This book is a collection of many powerful poems expressing romantic and spiritual love interspersed with beautiful abstract art in vivid colours.

A collection that has broken the cocoon of the poet and has metamorphosed her into a dynamic writer. The entire collection is like a conversation she wishes to have with her soul, those words which will remain unsaid if she doesn't carve them into poetry.

Every poem is short and effortless to read and understand the true feelings of the poet. The poems are flowing and so will you flow along.

The poems are rather a peep into the depths of otherwise standing firm on her grounds, a woman I know, who inspires many others around her each day and this time she has brought forth the most lamenting poems that sit gently over the soul.

Sweta experienced the angst of transition and chronicled her thoughts and emotions in poetry.

This collection displays those poems in a thoughtful series of themes that will take you from the depths of despair and uncertainty to the heights of hope.

Each poem has been carefully paired with photography to enrich the experience. It's a symphony of stimuli that's sure to take you on an emotional journey through the good and bad of the human heart.

- **DR.KCS MEHTA**

FOREWORD

BY

PRINCIPAL, ARMY PUBLIC SCHOOL, RAIWALA

Sweta has come a long way with this beautiful compilation of her heart prints in the form of this book called Bespoke

She is an amazing person with perfection in everything she does.

A great teacher whose dedication to her students and work has no bound...

I have always seen her loved and Respected by her students in whose young minds she has succeeded to leave life time impressions.

A doting mother to her daughter Naina and the life partner of an army officer Colonel Aditya Srivastava SC,SM. Sweta fits in all roles beautifully.

I have felt the most positive vibes in her ways of handling relationships and social obligations.

She is a master of her subject that she teaches i.e. Geography. But she seldom ceases to surprise me with her artistic talents and I can only appreciate and love her ways to make every work that she does so amazing and outstanding.

This book is a marvel and another addition to her multitalented personality. It's journey starts in her heart and soul and flawlessly she is able to pen down her emotions in beautifully decorated words and phrases and succeeds to enrich her readers with a great satisfaction of identifying themselves too with few situations.

I'm so happy for you dear Sweta, may this be just a beginning of the great heights and targets that you have set for yourself to achieve.

My Best wishes and compliments to Sweta

God bless!

- **CAPTAIN DIKSHA SHARMA (RETD)**

FIRST LOVE

Isn't it true that first love is always precious. To love without condition, by itself is simply like a string of pearls which forms a beaded necklace around the neck but it adds beauty to even the onlookers eyes Pure and perfect like stars in daylight. If you have ever felt in love before, you will agree like my poem, first love makes your feet no longer touch the ground...

1

FIRST LOVE

The season of love is here,
Just as a drop of dew
Settles on the windowpane,
I worship your love,
Like a seafaring vessel,
Moving far into the waves
Traversing the wide oceans,
my heart races as it reaches the shore.

And love like daisies has
Filled my garden with colours
There is laughter in the air
In my day and night,
Love like a blossom
Is fragrant and fine,
It is that infinite light
That helps the eyes to see.

It is the season of love
And my heart shines
Like the fresh essence of
A first touch in a young heart
As the first love blooms like
Flowers in heavens pleasant garden
My feet no longer touch the ground.

COUNTING THE DAYS

A period of separation from your beloved is a very difficult phase in life. It can feel like an unfathomable depth and an unimaginable pining of the heart .Its like a halo that surrounds you with your beloveds presence in everything you see. Sometimes you wish that it was not just a mirage and it was not just not a dream. A day in waiting is a long one, but what if your wishes are answered, and you turn to find him right infront of you !

2

COUNTING THE DAYS

I heard you sing to the wind today
And my heart, silently stood it's place,
When I did turn to see your face,
You weren't there,
But the winds embraced.....

Like a rhythm of my heart
The heavens have heard me
Call your name.
When I felt your touch
In the wind today
And just for a while it was
A love story...
When I turned to look for you,
You weren't there,
But the winds embraced....

When I closed my eyes,

To feel this warmth
I heard your voice, with the falling rain.
It was in a moments frame
As I overheard the valley
Sing your name
Once again it felt that
The heavens had
Caught me make a wish…
when I did turn to hear your voice,
You weren't there,
But the winds embraced…

Till eternity, I hold you
Close to my heart
And wait for us to meet again,
So what if the winds do sway,
They are for now,
But when I saw your eyes,
In the glass pane today,
Shining bright and black
I turned to see you,
My heart had skipped a beat
And I couldn't believe
But ,you were there !!

SPACES BETWEEN US

Though I can't say much about how one feels about living far from the ones you really love these days, but what I know for sure is that in our times, it was really difficult to even communicate. There were distances and duties, but the heart still ruled and it kept us waiting for a chance to be near our beloved. When finally we reached where we wanted to be, years had passed, and perhaps even changed a part of you and me ...for those who believe, that love remains but love changes with time ....

3

SPACES BETWEEN US

Between me and the
Blessed unpaved trail,
Between the mountains and the bushes
I kept watching you leave.

Far and into a distance
Till I walked close
To the waterfall
Cascading rivulets
Into prism drops
To colour my world.

Between the moment
You had left and
Between how my heart
Pined to be with you
The waterfall plunged

Deep and loud
Over the rocks,
Now cold , placid, yet wild.

Between the moments
I climbed the stairs
And breathed in between….
I reached where I saw you leaving.
I left the stream behind
But my heart still
Searches for you !!

A SERENE HEART

This poem reflects a part of my persona because I am a deep thinker, who loves to be quiet and stay away from the glitz , even if opportunities emerge, I accept only to fulfill my role, it's my fascination to trace nature, and to let it take its course.

4
A SERENE HEART

A serene heart
Like waves submerging
Deep in some music,
Some lyrics, mellifluous

Shimmying from a shy nook
To create
Sounds from the waves
To sparkle some more
Just to let me hear my song.

For now
The tranquil touch
Of memories from my past
Have flowed in the rhythm

Of music of the rain
With a dulcet voice,

And now I see the ripples
Dancing with the waves
Shining along the edges of my boat.

TEHRI

Just a few lines portraying the intensity of Tehri. It's a reservoir of water, but also a keeper of lost hopes, dreams, beliefs and homes of almost forty villages that have got submerged under this lake. In the moments when you are there ,the beauty of the place can stir the soul, but its water still reflects the clock tower that perished along with all that was, now as its past.

5

TEHRI

Tehri ,like an adorned princess,
So complete in grace,
In path unforeseen,
She offers herself again and again.
In her genteel playful ways,
She blesses everything with her touch.

With more than forty villages
submerged below her,
Time persists
Though the clock tower perished !
So in occasional angrier times,
She outbursts her emotions,
In ravage and destruction,
But only to forgive, and lest we forget.

Slowly as the vision fades away,

Imperfect thoughts hovering in the minds
I try to trace its origins
And softly hear the winds
Bring the story to me.

STREAM

Who doesn't like the sight of a beautiful river ? But to reach its bed, one has to travel,through the mountains and the plains. As you trace its path ,the journey entices you with hopes of a perfect future especially when you are close to the perfect stream.

6

STREAM

Winding road in
The forests so deep,
To travel through the woods
And to listen to the breeze,
Where you will find the time go slow,
And the nature's tunes turn mellow,
Where you will find your solitude
In the dancing leaves,
In the bending trees ....

Sometimes across the bushy hollows
There is some place
Close to the fair stream
That whispers of the
Lovely land long ago….
So I move along,
Enchanted like a child

With some fears and
Many a dreams,
Of losing my way and finding my soul….

And so my thoughts
Linger on as I wander
Along the bends and curves of the
Rustic roads ....
Where there is stubbornness
of some wet trees
And where there is a
Brilliant flowing stream.

GANGES

Haridwar is one of the oldest towns in human civilizations, unique for its Ghats and Mansions by the Ganges which descends here from the mountains to the plains. It is scenic and radiant of beauty. Even during the rains , its waters turn muddy ,but the painted walls along its banks still can't match the beauty of the youthful river.

7

GANGES

Roll on fair Ganges
I have seen you descend
From the mountains to the plains
For my heart was yearning to take this scenic route…
Serenading life's moments in
Every path you turn,
Through veering rain and
That farfetched mist which
Somehow veils the day…

So roll on fair Ganges,
You are my hearts faith
For I know you will flow
A thousand miles
Beyond the listless lands,
Mounting up along the musical chants..

Drifting and quenching my soul…
Shining beneath the sun
Turbid yet bright like eternity ….

So roll on fair Ganges
I have seen you descend
From the mountains to the plains
For you are the calm
My weary soul yearns
So I watch you flow along
The painted walls,
Somehow still against the borrowed beauty
Of the river alone,
For I know now Ganges,
You are on your way to meet the sea ,
Muse on revered
With a poets eye !!

THE JUNGLE

The place where I currently stay is amidst a deep forest, along a blessed river that flows by my house. As if I was God's chosen child ,I got the opportunity to learn how the nature works in its magnificence. On one particular day I saw a herd of SAMBARS cross the river together, they waited for each other, and made sure none is left behind alone. This is what I have penned about.

8

THE JUNGLE

Because nature needs no filter,
The jungle to me is an
Extraordinary place,
Full of mystique and grace,

In all its splendor,
Mystery abounds,

It's an enigma and
Nature is incharge
Of birds singing as loud as can be,
And a bevy of the wild,

Crossing the river
At the end of daylight….

All of this is,

A sight to behold,

A trek to take,
A jungle I know.

MOONRISE

Sharad Purnima or a full moon night is a cultural celebration across regions.The lunar face is bright but sometimes its shadow is strong and can steal upon its timid and farfetched shine. so moonrise is a poem that brings a union between the moon, its shadow and me!

9

MOONRISE

So when the moon
Turns to play with the clouds,
Its shadow steals upon,
The moons timid shine
Just existing in its own orbit,
Pulling through the tides,
Watching alone this moonrise,
It feels we are three,
The moon, its shadow and me !

So when the moon
turns to play with the clouds ,
its shadow is calm
And subdued in a
Dark silhouette,
Following the bends of
The sky and tides,

The shimmery gleams
Line mystic spaces
Swaying a natures lullaby
And it feels alone we are three,
The moon, its shadow and me !

UNREASONABLE

If love was like a drop of water, I carry a whole ocean , but it's not always still and waiting for the wind to carry it forward. Sometimes the storms rise from within. Ofcourse, the nature's furore is never welcome to all , it causes a commotion .However stomp it must, otherwise there will be no clear day. Being unreasonable is that part of my life.

10

UNREASONABLE

And why should one
Not be unreasonable?
Why else are we here?
If we can't dream of just

Being ourselves,
To move towards the unknown,
To weave a new tale
Each and every day.

And why should one
Not be unreasonable?
To make room for surprises
And to take life as it comes,

To leave some questions
Without any answers.

Perhaps we should be !
Why else are we here ?

VALLEY OF FLOWERS

I believe that natures beauty cannot be captured in a camera, sometimes you can feel it in words but what the eyes see ,is like a joy at another level. When your trip ends ,you can take away pictures and keepsakes ,but the ethereal and picturesque reality remains where one can only go back to experience again.

11

VALLEY OF FLOWERS

It's time to wrap
My trip from the hills,
But I wish I could show all
That my eyes have seen
In the Queen of Hills
Amidst the valley of flowers
Exquisite and unpretentious
Fragrant wildflowers,
Rolling down the hills,

Between the walls and the pavements,
Holding violets against
The blue of the sky,
Just bundled to no order.
No rhyme ,
Like jumbled blossoms
Sowed far and wide.

Some pretty enough to
Bunch a fable,
And others run wild to
Engross the soil.

It's time for me to wrap
My trip to the hills
But I wish I could show all
That my eyes have seen,
In the golden hours
I spent trekking by the rills,
Fragrant wildflowers,
Clinging towards the edge of the hills,
Growing freely facing the sky,
Living untamed in natures choice of colours,

Like Dandelions
In a celestial dream,
Or the Elfwort
Healing an arrows tear.
Some just stuck close to the soil,
And others growing alone,
All this while !
It's time for me to wrap

My trip from the hills,
But I wish I could show all ,
That my eyes have seen.
Along the ridges,
Perched close to the earth,
Bright and magnificient
Fragrant wildflowers.
Spreading far in a riot of colours

Dozens piled in a bushy maze,
Forming a memory in the
Onlookers gaze…
In a feeling of awe,
Not afraid to bend over the rocks,
In bunches often trampled upon
But shining like the Cosmos flower.

My trip to the hills
Has come to an end
But I wish I could show all
That my eyes have seen

All along the slopes on the hills,
In the deep foliage,

Like heavens own flowerbed
I have seen exotic yet
Fragrant wildflowers.

FRANGIPANI

Frangipani is my best loved blossom, because it symbolizes strength, growth and an everlasting bond between married couples. It's a pleasing and alluring flower that is about self love and to see the white Plumeria swaying is all it takes to set young hearts ablaze.

12

FRANGIPANI

The winds string a Ukulele
And the leaves sway

In this music fiesta,
It's like a fine soiree

If you just close your eyes
You could hum a tune,

To the pearly white
Scintillating petals,

As it begins to drizzle,
The soft raindrops,

They whisper soulful emotions
Making a beautiful

Pastel sound,
Yes , it's like a

Fine soiree !!

FINE THINGS IN LIFE

In our fast paced lives, we sometimes even forget to take a small breather for ourselves. Not finding time to show appreciation to little things that can make you feel better, make you be thankful and grateful to experiences that actually validate your life. My poem is a celebration of such fine things in life. Have a look !

13

FINE THINGS IN LIFE

And I know it's the fine things
In life that count,
Like closing your eyes and
Facing the breeze
And feeling it deep
Along your soul,
To find the wind stirring your heart,
Have you ever felt It,
Just tousle
Through your hair !!
Till you open your eyes
And live the zenith.

And I know It's always the fine things
In life that count,
Like standing on tiptoes,
And reaching out to the day mist,

And tracing the mild Petrichor
It's like a fragrant deliverance,
Through this haze.
Have you ever felt this rain
Drench your soul !!

Because I know it's always the fine things
In life that count,
Like reaching out
To the source divine
And facing the sun to feel its warmth
For it is an enigma,
I wonder how it heals !
All I know is that
It's always the fine things
In life that count.

SECRET WATERFALL

A waterfall is more than a flowing sensation , it is a transience of youth. Its beauty only adds up when one waits by a bridge ,watching over its cascades, and feels a drop of rain in her eyes. Almost like a mild conversation, the Secret waterfall is looking for answers, because days in waiting pass so fast, but does the beloved also pine for you ?

14

SECRET WATERFALL

So when it rains,
My dear, do you ever wait to see,
The tiny pearls drizzle from the sky,
Sometimes turning,
Sometimes pouring,
And at times,
Settled just in your eyes !

So when it rains,
My dear, do you also see
How the tiny pearls,
Just mingle in the old Brooke,
Sometimes flowing,
Sometimes hurdling,
And at times being part
Of this secret waterfall !

So when it rains,

My dear, and if you are just
By the river alone,
Do you also wait to see
The setting sun,
Sometimes glowing,
Sometimes flaring,
And at times truly beaming the skyline !

And so when it rains,
My dear, do you also
Wait to hear the pearly drops
Echo in the mountains,
Sometimes gently,
Sometimes loud,
And at times it sounds,
Like the magic surrounds !

And so when it rains ,
My dear, do you also
Wait for me by the valleys
When you walk,
Sometimes tenderly,
Sometimes enduring,
And at times just
Like the heavens have met the Earth !

ON A WINTER DAY

Winter is a starkly beautiful season, filled with morning dew, bright daylight and frosty chills by the time its night. The sun is the season's chevalier whose ardor brings comfort. Infact the winter is the time to be tasteful and yuletide appropriate, bringing joy and gaiety to one and all.

15
ON A WINTER DAY

There must be something about
The sunshine that exists,
Beautifully within the day
That warms my skin,
With the lightest rays of touch.

There must be something
About the still moist winds
Which leave the grasses wet,
To give my feet,
A soft pathway,
Within the smell of this soft cold.

There must be something
In the season,
That it still stirs my life,
To follow its gale,
A little something extra,

A little something beautiful

BIRDS OF PASSGAE

This is a poem about a flock of birds I saw migrating over the river and across the ridges .I was mesmerized by their formations and undulating feats in the air. I wondered how lacking our own sense of union could be, and I wished these birds which fly across the continents, flapping their wings could teach us to make our journeys a bit more easier

16
BIRDS OF PASSGAE

Our longing for a clear sense
Comes with every bird spotted
Count by count.

The dark spotted- V ,
Shows how lacking our
Direction is,
How unsteady our
Concept of union is.

Our inherent pull,
That causes us to shift,
Like seasons,
Just like the sun does
With the daily sky,

The flock of birds,
Following the skyward pulse,

Fathom this Earth,
In this infinite orbit,
And we watch as
Mute beholders!

WHISPERS

The rivers whisper, but only the trees and flowers can hear. The soft undertone persists in the brightness of the blooms…purple, yellows and pink…conspicuous in the season ,especially when it is spring in my garden. It's about my love for having a lawn full of flowers.

17
WHISPERS

Its spring in my garden
And I see the whisper
Of the mountains,
Tiptoe to the surface of
The riverbanks.

The soft motion of the trees
Waving their branches,
Like open arms,
With joyous notes
Within the wind,
Has hushed the plumage
Of the birds flocking by.

In adoration
We welcome the spring,
Like tranced creatures'
Waiting to see

All that is bright and beautiful

ANXIOUS LOVE

Insecurity can be felt in any relationship because when it sets in, it can be overwhelming .Most people in love go through the phase, because when you first fall in love, it is about perfection, it is only with time ,that it's intensity tries to entice ,it may also become palpable. Could love ever be without any questions ?

18
ANXIOUS LOVE

What if things were never
As they were supposed to be,
Would we be now,
How we used to be,
Would we accept the
Little things in life,
Even on a day ,
That the sun didn't shine .

And what if we got
Everything that we ever needed,
Would we all be ,
Filled with gratitude,
What if there was no difference,
Between you and me,
Would we still always,
understand each other.

What if there was
No laughter ,no joy,
Could we still endure
The ups and downs in this life,
Would there be anything,
Without our love,
That we could still enjoy ?

A LONG DRIVE

This composition is a poetic thought about changing landscapes one witnesses as we travel along the open roads in excitement and in fervor. It's a long descent from the hills to the plains where now a river flows and in between it's about the marvels of the world .

19
A LONG DRIVE

A landscaped canvas of golden rocks ,
Glistening with beams of sunlight,
Side by side
Encased within the winding roads,
Sculpted like ravenous cuttings
By rampart hands we drive.

Look far along the horizon,
A sodden countryside ,
In a sudden rout has turned
incandescent,
By a changing wind,
Not always ,though sometimes
The sun does ignite
this cloudy autumn.

Rolling past now the traverse fields,
A canopy appears amidst branches of trees,

Butterflies romance in jocund mood,
Rushing hither- tither,
In the shadow of thick clouds,
Buzzing with the bees ,
Amidst the Guras trees.

In an hour of watchfulness and insight,
It has been a soft low descent,
It's like a light breeze that has
disturbed the water.
Painted with colours stolen from
the rocks and leaves and fern,
Is the kingfisher concealed in a watery
disguise
Waiting to be seen,
And how it takes its flight.

SWEET SERENITY

Everyone has a favourite place at home. Mostly it's not a place that's built only within four walls and textured with cement. It is more like a spot where one shares good times and laughter. It was my luck that I found serenity by the rocks and white sands along a river bank.I wish I could keep this happy place with me forever.

20
SWEET SERENITY

I have a little picture in my heart,
Of what my slice of heaven looks like,
It's made up of white sand and blue waters,

Overbank rocks,
Like peace and calm in a vibrant heart.

I have a little reason to paint,
My share of paradise,
Its coloured like waves and winds,

Around the shore,
Like crayons spreading over an easel.

I have a little wish to make,
Only if I could keep with me forever,
This sight of the river below the branches

Where I love to sit,
My safe haven , this sweet serenity.

ALOHA BY THE GANGES

If you have ever travelled to Rishikesh, the beauty of Laxman Jhula and the Ganges flowing underneath is sure to catch your eyes, both adding reflections to each other. The place is an ultimate escape from the mundane, it stirs you spiritually and drives you to believe in persistence of the divine.

21
ALOHA BY THE GANGES

Just sit by and watch
The city lights
Hear the Ganges
Whisper and murmur
Bejeweled in reflections
You will be mesmerized
Looking at its arms
Embrace the shores.

Look a little far
And it grows and grows
Leaving you with a
Soft scent of the
Waters so pure
Shining still in the night
Like a sight so prompt
To delight.

It bedazzles the soul
That plunges for more
Of this rivers might
Gazing along the bridge
That arches from
Side to side
Bringing along a union
Of dark and light.

Hovering over the
Sharp bend
Over the Ganges
Look still a little further
You can see
That the river has flowed
But it has no end

A NOTE OF THANKS

Everything that is truly right for you will happen serendipitously. You may have to wait for the right time or the opportunity may come straight looking for you. Either ways there will be a spontaneous and obvious certainty and direction that will follow. For me writing my book was harder than I had imagined, but none of this would have been possible without the support and encouragement of my family. My brother ,Akash, whose pictures I have used to adorn my poems, and my sister, Navita, who helped me out with the expressions.

I wish to thank everyone who has ever said a positive and encouraging word to me.The love you have showered has brought me abundance in thoughts and wishes .It has helped me take this first leap.

Addie and Naina, I am nothing without you both.

PAPER2PUBLISH

Manan Verma's publishing company
Awarded by Uttarakhand Government

With Paper2Publish you can start your book publishing journey with just ₹1000. Paper2Publish Publishing can turn you into a published author in just 30 days.

You will be assigned a team by Paper2Publish who will help you with writing, editing, cover design, copyright, ISBN and everything you need to become a worldwide published author.

With the help of Paper2Publish Print on demand technology, you can now get as low as 30 books printed. Gone are the days of investing all your life savings in getting 500 books printed at once.

Paper2Publish team is more than happy to turn you into a worldwide published author in just 30 days.

Contact for more details:

+91-7417549575, Paper2publishing@gmail.com
Instagram: @paper2publish

Free session: www.paper2publish.com/free-bonus/

www.ingramcontent.com/pod-product-compliance
Lightning Source LLC
LaVergne TN
LVHW050421160826
845677LV00002BA/477
9789394450295